MEDITATIC

GW00706140

Bodel Rikys/Polair Publishing

meditation is...

the how

of the now

meditation is...

soft

eyes

mind

belly

meditation is...

soft mind

unwinding

opinions

rightwrong

thisandthat

youandme ♥

meditation is...

coming home

to the body

meditation is...

being held

by your own

heart radiance

meditation is...

riding

the breath

meditation is...

single focus

meditation is...

letting go

meditation is...

really tasting

the tea

meditation is...

letting the waves
of your mind
settle down

meditation is...

curling up with

a good mantra

meditation is...

simplicity

meditation is…

using the breath
to keep the mind
from straying

meditation is...

a light repose

on the object

meditation is…

spacious

meditation is...

being kind to your

own unkindness

meditation is...

wearing your heart

on your heart

meditation is...

a mirror

meditation is...

being a
connoisseur
of the here and now

meditation is...

a banana for

the monkey mind

meditation is…

being there

meditation is...

sunning yourself

from the inside

meditation is…

paying attention

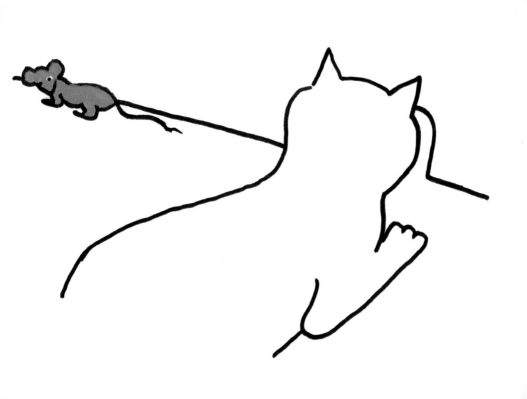

meditation is…

being satisfied

with what is

meditation is...

accepting the present

as a present

meditation is...

sitting with

the heart of things

meditation is...

feeling

the connection

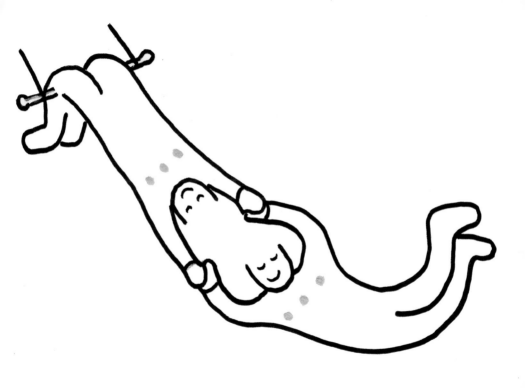

meditation is...

coming down

gently

meditation is...

the journey home

meditation is...

resting in the place betw

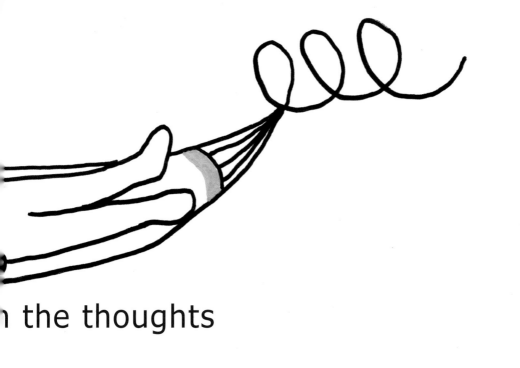

the thoughts

meditation is…

the beginning

the end

...

meditation is...
first published October 2007 by Polair Publishing, P O Box 34886,
London W8 6YR and printed by Cambridge University Press
A catalogue record for this book is available from the British
Library / ISBN 978-1-905398-14-0 / © Bodel Rikys 2007

For Phillip

Bodel Rikys is an artist, illustrator and teacher of
meditation, based in London: www.N16health.com.

The popular Polair Guides series includes
why meditation works/James Baltzell/ISBN 978-1-905398-06-5
along with titles on yoga and alternative therapies, while Polair's
longer list extends to astrology, literature, the environment and
self-help. Write to the address above for a free catalogue or
check us out at
www.polairpublishing.co.uk